A Rose

for the

Heart of Life

Selected Poems

Hussein Habasch

inner child press, ltd.

Credits

Author
Hussein Habasch

Editor
hülya n. yılmaz, Ph.D.

Cover Painting
Ahmed Kleige

Cover Design
William S. Peters Sr. &
inner child press, ltd.

Translators
Muna Zinati
Sinan Anton
Azad Akkash
Norddine Zouitni
Jawad Wadi
Hewa Habasch
Mohammad Helmi Rishah
Margaret Saine
Solara Sabah

General Information

Hussein Habasch
A Rose for the Heart of Life

1ˢᵗ Edition: 2021

Publisher Information:

Inner Child Press
innerchildpress@gmail.com
www.innerchildpress.com

ISBN-13: 978-1-952081-45-3 (Inner Child Press, ltd.)

$ 18.95

Disclaimer from the Editing Department

In order to maintain the poet's authentic voice and the original work of the translators, this publication has not undergone the full standard scrutiny of editing. Please take time to indulge this collection for the author's own creativity and aspirations to convey the uniqueness of his written art and its materialization through translations.

hülya n. yılmaz, Ph.D.
Director of Editing Services

This book is dedicated to all my friends around the world.

Table of Contents

The Poetry

Table of Contents . . . *continued*

Table of Contents . . . *continued*

Table of Contents . . . *continued*

Table of Contents . . . *continued*

Table of Contents . . . *continued*

Table of Contents . . . *continued*

Table of Contents ... *continued*

Epilogue

Preface

Exile, Poetry, the World and I

The Exile of Languages

Being born Kurdish to Kurdish parents who only know Kurdish from God's numerous languages, I wanted – just like all children – to play, study, learn, and spell my first letters in my mother tongue. Instead, I found myself in a maze of other languages in front of a language where I didn't know one letter from another: Arabic. A few years later, the child who grew inside of me day after day asked himself, "Why are you studying and learning this strange language instead of the language of your mother, father and grandfathers?" Time and awareness gave a frank answer to that question: the Kurdish language was and still is forbidden in Syria – except when it's spoken at home with the family.

The Kurdish culture is forbidden and persecuted in Syria. Writing in Kurdish is forbidden since there are no schools, institutions, or universities that teach it or include in their curriculum. Therefore, the only option that I was given was to master Arabic and educate myself step-by-step by studying, reading, and writing. This is precisely what happened. And now, I am here, writing my poems in this foreign language with a high imagination and an infatuation, which is incomparable except for my infatuation with poetry itself, and at a depth that emulates so many fellow poets and writers of this language. In this context, I would like to add the fact that I learned to read and write my mother tongue in exile, in Europe, where I am allowed to write in Kurdish my poems, texts, and obsessions.

The Homeland's Exile

An Arabic journalist wants to ask me about my reasons for living in Germany. He will publish the entire conversation in an Arabic press; and yet, the answer to that controversial question will end up being deleted and I do not know why! I will answer, *I was forced to run away from Syria. At that time, I told myself, 'Run away before you commit suicide, go crazy, go to jail, starve, or the fire of life and hope that burns inside of you goes out. Leave this country, which has turned into nothing more than a disintegrated corpse, a corpse that has no value of love, freedom, beauty, or human dignity; leave it before despair gnaws on your heart and soul; leave it before all of your dreams pass away'.* For these reasons, I found myself in a new place of exile, an exile from where I long for my birthplace. Whenever I hear its sad news, I appreciate my exile and stay devoted to it. Living in exile is difficult, but living in my country of birth is harder. Poetry moistens the hardness of it all. But I would like to say here very clearly, that my only country was and still is Kurdistan, and Syria was and is still occupying part of my native country and the place from which I came from!

Poetry is a Perpetual Fever

Poetry is a smooth speech, which is not completed without the use of misery; pain, misery, and suffering are poetry's fundamental springs, its source of existence. Poetry is therefore a creation and a birth that cannot exist without real suffering. Even in poetry about joy and love there are hints of suffering, anxiety, pain, sadness, and misery; these mentions are inevitable.

In literature, and specifically in poetry, I am tempted to stay in a heated room all of the time, a room which is heated by fantasy and insanity, a room which allows me to venture into extremism – as the famous German philosopher, Nietzsche, once stated. Poetry cannot coexist with coldness. It cannot live in a cold room, with the coldness of mind. It is the son of fantasy and insanity; it asks us all to stay for its sake, in a constant state of fever and hotness. I write poetry to steal myself away from myself and to make the dream more passionate than anything I have ever seen, to bring my insanity to the level of a grand wonder. Poetry, this creature that is unequaled to anything else in existence, can make me sacrifice everything for its sake, the sacred and the profane. From time to time, I ask the person within me, *You, poet, who is inside of me, were you loyal to poetry's lesson? Did you sacrifice enough for its sake?* And then I answer myself, *I am trying with all of my power, cells, and blood that flows through my veins.*

Poetry and the World

Poetry cannot heal humanity's pains or liberate nations from injustice or despotism; it is not one of poetry's duties to lead revolutions or carry out justice and equality to the world. Poetry cannot stop humiliation and pain, which people are exposed to everywhere. Yet, poetry is like a scream in the face of this epidemic that spreads here and there; a scream in the face of wars, jails, killing, violence, cruelty, racism, exile, and destruction, all of which covers the universe; a scream that can embrace the world from all of its sides and spread moments of warmth, love, and liberty through its veins. At first, this poetic scream should be written well, in a powerful imagination, in a charm, miracle, love, and insanity; otherwise, it will fall in the well of antipathy. The world of poetry has a different shape from the world without it. If the world wears poetry, it will be resurrected from the ashes into the light, from dullness into delicacy . . .

Hussein Habasch

Translations by

Muna Zinati

A Rose for the Heart of Life

A Rose for the Heart of Life

Our madness to draw
Our madness to write
Our madness to leave every day
A rose for the heart of life
Our madness won't win, my love!

Their madness to fight
Their madness to kill
Their madness to aim every day
A bullet to the heart of life
Their madness will win, my love!

We will be defeated, my love.
I know that.
They will conquer, my love.
You know that.

But regardless, we will draw,
Write and leave every day
A rose for the heart of life.

Five Women in Black Scarves

Five women in black scarves
Lined up in front of the missing people's desk!

The first said,
I am looking for my husband's name,
Missing for two years.

The second said,
I am looking for my son's name,
Missing for five years.

The third said,
I am looking for my father's name,
Missing for four years.

The fourth said,
I am looking for my sweetheart's name,
Missing for three years.

The fifth said,
I am looking for my country's name,
Missing for hundreds of years!

The five women came out of the line,
Collapsed on each other
As a tent; a horrible massacre happened upon it
And started to strike and cry!

The Red Snow

The snow comes down white
Covering all the mountains with whiteness
The snow comes down white
On Kurdistan's mountains too
But it soon turns red!

The Embrace

When the two lovers heard
The fighter planes roar,
They embraced each other.
When the sound approached more,
They embraced each other more.
When the bombing and destruction began,
They embraced each other tightly.
Now they stand in an embrace in eternity.

The Lazy Pupil

They told him,
Draw a school;
He drew an amusement park.

Draw a teacher;
He drew a rose.

Draw a lake;
He drew a swan.

Draw autumn;
He drew a green bud.

Draw the sky;
He drew his father.

Draw the earth;
He drew his mother.

Each time,
The lazy pupil
Was drawing his heart.

A Dialogue

What is happiness, father?
It's a bird that forgot his feathers
and wings in the desert, son!

What is life, father?
It's a boiled egg. We are in it, son!

What is human, father?
He is an acrobatic dancer on the edge of the abyss, son!

What is isolation, father?
It's separating the soul from all the world's aspects, son!

What is love, father?
They said, it's a healthy sickness, son!

What is future, father?
It's a sun that only shines on the lucky ones, son!

What are tears, father?
It's a rain that missed its way, son!

What is bravery, father?
It's a ball of fire that rotates inside the heart, son!

What is pain, father?
It's a shirt we wear from our birth to our death, son!

Weeping

She wept in the morning
She wept at noon
She wept in the evening
In the morning, she lost a son
At noon, she lost another
In the evening, she lost the last of family
The next morning, they cried for her
At noon, they cried for those who were crying for her
In the evening, there were no remaining cries
The whole town was swamped with blood.

Regrets

In Paris
I had a great regret
Because I did not do
What my wound mate did, Gérard de Nerval
Or as my mate in despair did, Paul Celan
I regretted
Oh, the Mirabeau Bridge
I regretted
I regretted because
I did not answer the call.

A Dark Mood in Paris

I want death
A fast death
Not a gasp or breath in it
Not a sad pulse in it
A silent death
Without a cry or a consolation
Not a majestic say in it
I want death
Befitting a poet
Who cannot bear life anymore.

Forgetfulness

When a thorn saw the hungry through her eyes,
It was very sad, and it said:
I wish I were a wheat field.
The forest trees heard it and said:
We wish our fruits were wheat.
The rain also heard it and said:
I wish my rain drops became wheat,
Dripping through hungry bellies.
The dirt heard it too and said:
I wish the whole of me became wheat.
Even the stones, when they heard it, said:
We wish our hearts became wheat.
The human heard it and said:
I wish . . .
But he forgot to finish his sentence!

O Love, O War!

O war,
O endless filth,
Leave here, go to hell!
We want to write
Love poems
Without your unpleasant odor penetrating through them.
We want to kiss our wives, sweethearts, and mistresses
Without hearing your noise around us.
We want to die from love, from love alone!

I am in exile, and the war is at its height.
Oh God, how much I missed your small wars, my love,
Your wars in which my heart and I were happy victims.

Go on, be a little crazy, have a little fun;
Or if you want, ruin my mood with your huge dose of
    grouchiness.
I don't want to think about this nasty war which is taking
    place in my homeland.

This war is a machine, grinding the meat of love
And crushing its bones with no mercy!
With love, we will grind war's bones and eliminate it!

It seems, this war has no end.
Come, let us plant trees and sleep, cuddling up next to
    them until they grow.

Don't say, you have no time.
This war will drag for a long time.
I don't want our love to be defeated.

The lover was saying to his sweetheart,
I will kiss you until dawn.

Now he says,
I will kiss you until this war explodes from rage.

Put your hand on my forehead.
Distract this war that almost crushes my head.
With love, we will crush its head!

War doesn't like to pause,
Doesn't like holidays nor laziness.
It likes work, and it does it with the utmost devotion and
    dedication;
And the more its work pays off,
The more it grows passionate, energetic, and moves
    forward.
With love, we will stop it on its track; yes, we will
    stop it . . .

War doesn't listen, doesn't obey nor answer to anybody.
It goes to its goal as a fatal bullet goes directly to the heart
    of life.
We will return the favor twice as hard.

In war,
We won't build a house; we won't put any stone over
    stone.
We will write poems and sing songs.
Nothing enrages war more than poems and songs.

I will go to war.
"And what will you do there?"
I will kill war!

"What do you do in wartime?"
I write love poems.
"What else?"
I hold on more to love!

We Will Not Survive

We will not survive.
Our sins are plentiful and our loads are massive.
We left everything unleashed.
We didn't care about what was happening around us
While we neglected our humanity.
We approved war and we forbade love.
We scattered dirt on beauty, and we left
The ghoul of ugliness roaming everywhere.
We thrusted daggers on each other's chest
And we no longer know how to plant a tree or water,
A parched flower.

The Père Lachaise Cemetery

I saw not one dead person
In the Père Lachaise Cemetery
I saw only proud tombstones
Raising their heads to the sky
And a small squirrel playing on Pilzac's shoulder
And listening with delicate ears
To the sorrowful singing
Coming from the Piaf family tomb.
At that moment, I imagined
I heard Edith Piaf sing her great song:
"Non, je ne regrette rien."

Health

In the early morning,
the man runs
to build his muscles
and maintain his health.

In the early morning,
the woman runs
for the flowers to bloom
and to maintain nature's health.

Intimacy

On the Rhine
A man and a woman
A male and a female dog . . .
The woman holds the man's hand.
She brings her lips closer to his breath.
With desiring eyes, the dog looks
At the female dog's hazel eyes.
The river is running happily.

Cruel Outsiders

We were prosperous
We weren't missing anything
Cruel outsiders came from a faraway place
And they seized everything!

They stole our wealth
They milked our cows
They tore out our chickens' feathers
They rode our horses
They detached our doors
They violated the sacredness of our homes
They confiscated all our assets.

We weren't bad peasants
We were planting fertile lands
With experience inherited from grandfathers and fathers.

We were managing our wealthy treasures
Olives, wheat, grain, vegetables and fruit-bearing trees
With our fullest competence.

We were gathering winter supplies
Wheats, grits and olive oil
Raisins, almonds and dried figs
From the abundant crops that our rich land
Brought to us generously.

We were milking our cows' udders
Which were full of fresh milk, from which we obtained
Margarine, butter, and yogurt
And fresh cheese which never left our breakfast table.

We were riding horseback smoothly
And we were moving as arrows towards the vast prairies,
Hunting rabbits, deer and fatty birds.

At night, we were returning to our homes and families,
Happy, cheerful and wholesome.

We were prosperous
But cruel outsiders came from a faraway place
And they seized everything
Everything, even the air we breathe.

Fabiola

Fabiola,
Whenever you pass the fields in your embroidered clothes,
A rainbow emerges beyond the hills,
A deer runs by the riverbank,
A bird flies,
A cloud lands on the green mound's shoulder.

Fabiola,
Whenever you unfold your silky shawl
And toss your ivory dice,
The flowers bloom on maidens' laps,
Lucks pour into their hearts.
From above, the moon of love shines for them.

Fabiola,
Whenever you open your arms to embrace
And release your hair for the wind's kisses,
The wood bracelets clank,
The earrings swing in butterflies' ears
And the yearning's string dangles,
Like a light breeze from the heart of life.

Fabiola,
Why, when you step
And the gypsy's beauties with you step on some place,
Do the clouds laugh their white laugh,
The face of the earth becomes greener,
And the flowers of hopes bloom on lovers' collars?

Four Trees

They cut four trees
They made a cradle from the first one
They made a lover's bed from the second one
They made a cane for an old man from the third one
They made a chair for the king's palace from the fourth one
Despite the poverty,
The first, second and third trees
Were very happy
Despite the wealth and the beauty of the king's palace,
The fourth tree was very sad.

The Use of Love

All know the earth is round
No doubt it rotates
But they do not know
That the lover's heart is what makes it round
And the strength of their love
Is what makes it rotate.

Manuela, the Mulatto

Manuela, the mulatto brags about her short dresses
And her bare legs which shine like marbles
Under the sun's ray.
She opens three buttons of her shirt;
Two from above, to show her ample bosoms
And the third from bottom, so her round navel will shine
Like the face of the sun.
She wears red high-heel shoes,
Walks elegantly on the street like a princess
Coming out of mythologies.
Heads roll after her big behind . . .
Pedestrians, merchants, loungers, bikers
And the fast car-drivers!
She is being followed by lusty eyes from all directions.
The dice drops through the fingers
Of the most skilled player;
The rosary breaks off from the devout oldster;
The officer rubs his eyes with astonishment;
The drunk sways bewilderedly;
The blind hugs his cane and looks at it for a long time.
A wicked smile appears on Manuela, the Mulatto's face
And her legs' and three buttons' real thoughts say:
O street, go insane, and lose your mind more!
Tomorrow, I will put on a shorter dress.
Tomorrow, I will open another button!

A Mother's Effort

The door loved the window
The window loved the chair
The chair loved the table
The tree happily said: Thank God,
All my efforts and toil for my children
Were not in vain!

The Smiling Green Tree

One tree
Was always green and cheerful
They wanted to know her secret
They opened its heart
Found a bird
Flying from one artery to another
Building his nest in the middle.

Why Not?

A table wanted to become a chair
The chair said: Why not?
I always wished I had a sister.

Orsena, the Gypsy

You, Orsena, are very beautiful
Your beauty is supposed to be common to all as medicine
Everyone loves you
The neighborhood's trail and its dogs
The blackberries' fence and the tall poplar tree
The baker and the milkman
The tailor and the store owner on the street corner
The daisy and the flutter of butterflies' wings
The spring and the riverbank
The grape vine and the pine forest
The bicycle mender and the janitor
The school's guard and the concierge
The madman – insane – who persists on singing
The handicapped who keeps on complaining
The librarian who is drenched in books
The sad poet who lives in that room
Which overlooks your street
O, beautiful Orsena,
Everyone loves you like crazy
And they wait for your beautiful appearance eagerly
Don't hold back on them, Orsena!
Don't hold back your beauty which is supposed
To be common to all as medicine.

When Will You Come, Maria?

When will you come, Maria?
The rain is coming down heavily
And the heart is beating strongly
I will send an umbrella to you
I will prepare a heater for you.

When will you come, Maria?
The cold is severe
And the storm is strong
I will sew a sock for you
I will bring a coat for you.

When will you come, Maria?
The trail eagerly awaits your steps
And the door is ready for your finger's clicks
I will light a lantern for you
I will lift up a hat for you.

When will you come, Maria?
The longing is intense
And the desire is domineering
I will saddle a horse for you
I will order a coachman for you.

When will you come, Maria?
The stomach is empty
And the head is spinning
I will pour wine for you
I will prepare food for you.

I will wait for you, Maria, I will wait
Come, blow my birthday's candle

And get rid of the scary stillness for me
Don't be late, Maria!
Everything here is waiting for you
Everything, without an exception.

The Love of Two Trees

Two trees were madly in love with one another
The vindictive woodchopper
Cut their trunks off
He took them home
By chance, the two trees met in the fireplace
They embraced each other happily
And burned together.

Jealousy

The short tree told the long tree:
Enough already.
No matter how tall you get,
Your head will never reach the sky.
The tall tree bent over the short tree
And whispered to her:
Enough jealousy.
Enough.

In Bonn by the Rhine

In Bonn,
The Rhine talks to the ships
The ships talk to the Rhine
And I talk to both of them about you.

In Bonn,
The hours pass
The days pass
The months pass
The years pass
And I always pass toward you.

In Bonn,
The trees sway on the Rhine
The clouds rain over the Rhine
Cafés are crowded around the Rhine
And I sway with the trees,
Waiting for the rain,
Sit in cafés
And think of you.

In Bonn,
The life passes
The heart exhausts
The soul ages,
And you always remain
The life's wave,
Medicine for the heart,
Elixir for the soul
The Rhine passes
And I always stay, waiting for you.

In Bonn,
The lovers walk by the Rhine
Old people hit the ground with their canes
And lovely mothers fly kites with their children,
And I am looking at the lovers,
Mimicking the old people's funny movements,
Flirting with the lovely mothers
And waiting for you to come.

In Bonn,
The singers try out their vocal cords by the Rhine
The musicians play their violins
The dancers sway with the music
The dogs wag their tails,
And all the time, I am humming your name.

In Bonn
By the Rhine . . .
Always waiting for you
Always, always thinking of you.

The Snowman

I give you a sweater,
Gloves,
A hat,
A coat,
And a vast field of snow.
Make a man from the snow,
Put a carrot as his nose,
Two cherries for his eyes,
Your lipstick for his mouth.
Make the mouth smile,
Put the hat on,
Wrap your shawl tenderly around his neck.
If you can't find him a name,
Name him as me.
Then gather the neighbourhood kids
And tell them:
That is my sweetheart.
Come, play with him!

If You Ever Come Across a Sad Woman

If you ever come across a sad woman,
Do not say, "God be with you".
Do not say, "God help you relieve your grief".
No . . . No!
Do not tell her all that!
Embrace her with a warm heart.
Whisper to her,
"You are the most beautiful woman in the world.
Your eyes are more beautiful than all women's eyes.
When you smile, your flowery smile
Will bloom everywhere."
Then you will see
How love will shine through her eyes again;
How her spirit will thrive,
And how fast she will forget her sorrows.

Return the Favor

He had a house
Put its key in her hands
Take it, he said
It's your gift.

He had a horse
Put the saddle on its back
Come on and ride it, he said
It's your gift.

He had a gun
Put it on her shoulder
Take it, he said
It's also your gift.

She took the house
The horse
The gun.

She loaded the gun well
And fired two bullets to his heart!

A Tree's Dream

In a dream, a tree saw itself fly
All birds visited the tree in the morning
They gifted it with feathers and wings
And made it fly with them.

An Umbrella

The tree saw two nearly naked children
In the rain shivering from the cold
It ran
It ran fast toward them
Opened its leaves
Stood above them
Like an umbrella.

The Tree and the Necklace

A tree wanted a golden necklace for its long neck
The birds at that place gathered together
They lined themselves beside each other
And affectionately decorated the tree's long neck.

The Corona Era

Today,
I noticed the bird that sings all the time
In front of my window.
I didn't notice its singing before.

I noticed the three trees standing in front of my balcony
With their fresh rosy flowers, their tiny green buds
And their brown, hugging branches.
It never drew my attention before.

I noticed a swing and a thin wooden horse
At the children's playground in front of my balcony.
I didn't notice their existence before.

I noticed the Lilac trees at the nearby garden
That look like Walt Whitman's birthplace in New York.
I didn't notice their existence before.

I noticed two rows of stones
In front of my kitchen's window,
Five on both sides.
I didn't know that the stones have such magnificent beauty,
Even without cutting and carving.

I noticed my neighbor's clothesline.
Now I know the bright colors
Of her underwear and daywear.
I didn't know the beauty of her clothesline before.

I noticed the orchids hanging from
The old Polish lady's balcony.
I didn't know that she likes orchids
And that she is Polish before.

I noticed the two beautiful children playing
On the divorced Russian lady's balcony;
The complexion of one of them more of a black,
And the other more of a blond.
They told me that the first is from her African husband
And the second is from her Russian husband,
And now, she is dating her German sweetheart.
The neighbor's gossiping told me that.
I said, bless her heart.
Of course, I didn't know that before.

I noticed that my sixtieth German neighbor
Smokes on the balcony.
He smiled at me, and I smiled back.
We never did that before.

Two Trees

The tree under which two lovers sat
Had a bright smiling face
The tree in whose trunk the snake lived
Had always a pale sad face.

The Weeping Willow

They asked the weeping willow,
"Why are you always sad like that?"
Surprisingly, it answered: I am not sad.
"But why are your twigs and leaves always
Hanging and dripping tears?"
The willow tree laughed and said:
It's not as you imagine.
It's just so that I took a bath.

The Charcoal

A tree said:
If they broke all the pencils
Which wrote in the name of freedom,
I will burn one of my branches
And make it a charcoal, a chalk . . .
For the free to write on all walls of the world:
"Long Live Freedom!"

Coronavirus

What will we do if Corona visited us unawares
and it was in desperate need to use the toilet?
What if it asked to go to the toilet
and we don't have toilet paper?
How will it wipe its bottom?
How will it dry its sweat?
Nothing we can do!
Before we feel shameful and bow our heads
in embarrassment,
please enlighten us, we need a solution for this dilemma!

What if it asked for a sanitizer to sanitize its hands?
Where do we provide the sanitizer, after it suddenly
evaporated from the market and became a thing of the past?
What kind of infertility is this?
What kind of humiliation will we feel before it,
what kind of an embarrassment?

What if it asked us about gloves?
What will we say?
What kind of confusion and dismay are we getting into?
How will we justify the sudden vanishing of it?
Maybe we will say, it jumped out of the window, or
it ran away to keep the tidiness of its hand and palm.
A shy lie; so, probably we can save face before it.

What if it told us that it will visit the bacterial and
biological weapons' labs, and it is in a desperate need
for masks?
What will we say?
Do we say, it was stolen from the clinics and hospitals?
The merchants store it?

The tyrants use it to muzzle voices?
We don't know!
We don't know!
But we will cover our mouths with our palms,
mumbling in-between our confused fingers, and say,
we don't have masks,
we don't have . . .!

Hope

The woman hopes
to look beautiful in her own eyes.
The child hopes
to break his toys.
The homeless hopes
to find a shelter to sleep.
The drunkard hopes
to own a bottle of wine.
I hope to convince
the woman of her beauty,
the child to arrange his toys,
the homeless to find a shelter to sleep
and the drunkard to go to the bar.

A Tree's Grief

A tree was sad
Dust seized its greenish leaves
The rainfall was delayed
Oh heaven,
You are so stingy!

I Wish I . . .

When a tree saw
They make flutes from reeds,
It said:
I wish I were a reed.

Instead of a Race . . .

The poplar tree told the cypress tree:
Since our heads will never reach heaven,
Instead of this pointless race,
Let's hug each other.

Just Know That I Died

If one day you came and did not find me,
Just know that I am there.
If you came there and did not find me,
Just know, I am in a faraway place.
If you come that far and do not find me,
Do not be sad.
Plant a red rose deep in the heart of the earth,
And know that I died!

An Apology
Early 2013

I apologize to all the children
  whom I couldn't write about . . .
I apologize to all those who were martyred,
  killed, and died under the rubbles . . .
I apologize to all those who perished by sniper bullets,
  shot in cold blood . . .
I apologize to all those who were tortured with
  unmatched brutality . . .
I apologize to all those who were humiliated and imprisoned,
and to all those who remained in prison and under arrest . . .
I apologize to all those who migrated, were displaced and
  orphaned . . .
I apologize to all those who lost their schools, playgrounds,
  homes and warm beds . . .
I apologize to all those who live in refugee camps, outdoors,
and are caved in torn cloths and chilled bellies . . .
I apologize to all those who were wounded and lost
  important parts of their bodies, living with permanent
  impairments and disabilities . . .
I apologize to all those who drowned, were lost, missed,
  kept away and became an item on the list of the absent,
  the lost and the unknown . . .
I apologize to all those who died from hunger, cold, diseases,
  and lack of medicine, milk, and food . . .
I apologize to all those who lost their parents, brothers and
  sisters, friends and neighbours . . .
I apologize to all the Syrian children, those lost
  and those alive, whom I couldn't write about . . .
But here I am now, screaming at the top of my voice:
  O Almighty, how could they kill the children?
Exactly as before me Dostoyevsky screamed:
  "O Almighty, why do the children die? The difference
  between death and killing is so tremendous."

Bravery

Suddenly,
The tree extracted the axe's handle
And said: This is a part of me.
I do not want it to be a help to my enemy!

A Coffin

When they made a coffin out of a tree,
It had much pain
And was saddened;
But when they laid the martyr inside it,
It had a wonderful smile
And felt great pride.

Mercy

A bird built his nest
Atop a high tree.
The tree called God:
I beg you, God,
Do not send storms in my direction.

Hamzeh Alkhateeb

They didn't give him a chance to comb his hair
And to smile in the mirror,
Saying, how lovely you are, o little boy.
They didn't give him a chance to give his mother a kiss,
Asking her, how much is my love to you, mother?
They didn't give him a chance to curl his mustache,
Telling his father, I became a potent man, o father;
So, don't be scared for me.
They didn't give him a chance to meet his young love,
Telling her, when I see you, my heart beats
    like birds' wings
They didn't give him a chance to say goodbye
    to his friends,
Telling them, wait for me, o lads;
We will go to school together.
They didn't give him a chance to kick his football,
Telling it, I will score another goal when I come back.
They didn't give him a chance to grow, get married, and
    have children,
Naming his firstborn
Deraa or Houran.

*Hamzeh Alkhateeb: The child who protested the regime in Syria.
They savagely killed him, and severed his genitals.

The Tree and the General

A dirty general
Was back from the war
He wanted to rest under a tree
The tree ordered all its birds
To poop all together
On top of the criminal general's head!

Disappointment

A tree was disappointed with the rain.
It called: Oh God, I want an umbrella!

The Ascent

The boy who climbed the stairs
To inform neighbours
About the warplanes arriving
And the bombardment starting
Proceeded, ascending to heaven!

The Infant

The infant whom they removed out
From under the rubbles . . .
Harm didn't affect him much.
With purest innocence,
He was clinging to his mother's chest,
Sucking the remains of coagulated milk
That was left in her cold breast!

An Escape

From horror and the massive massacre,
The boy's tongue knotted.
With his trembling hands,
He recounted his bizarre tale of an escape.

The Gift

Each night, in his loneliness
On top of his roof,
He plucks up the stars from the sky
One by one,
Making a luminous necklace.
In the morning,
He offers it to you.

A Disguise

Before capturing her last breath,
She dyed with her dripping blood
Her child's body.
The child escaped the massacre!

Baba Ammer's Sparrows

Where are you, my son?
In heaven, father.
How did you arrive there, my son?
I flew with my little friends from Baba Ammer
And found myself there, father!

The Doll

The killer forgot to stab
The little girl's doll alongside her.
After the shock, the doll woke up.
It clutched its owner,
Refusing to be buried without her!

The Outrage

Why are you outraged, father?
The Houleh's children, my son . . .
What is wrong with them, father?
They were like you, playing . . .
And today, they were slaughtered, my son!
Who did this, father?
You will know it all tomorrow.
All of it, my son . . .

Urine

Is the urine
That the children released in terror
A moment before they've been captured by axes
And knives
Not more purified than the blood
That flows in the killer's vein?

A Race

The children were
Standing in one row . . .
The bullets didn't give them a chance
To start their race.
Now, no fright,
No bullets,
No killing . . .
They stand in one row,
Racing to eternity.

The Camera

The camera which was snapping photos
Of children's corpses
Was frightened by the horrible scenes.
With confused steps, it retreated backwards.
Heavy tears poured down
From the lens.

Deeply Weeping

The woman was deeply weeping
Not for her lost husband
Not for her demolished home either
Nor for her wasted property . . .
She was weeping
Because her baby was crying nonstop
From hunger,
And the poor woman didn't have any solution!

A Smile

The martyred child who was smiling
Wasn't smiling for the smile's sake only!
He was doing that to ease his mother's agony
And to relieve the terrible grief his death caused her.

A Comb

The little girl sat down
Combing her doll's hair
Humming a song for her
The treacherous bullets arrived
Combing her
Combing her family and home
Her cat and garden
Her swing, dreams, and her chants
Combing her neighbours
And her friends.

Tresmeh's Children

Tresmeh's children say:
Now, we don't want milk
We don't want bread
We don't want toys
We don't want new clothes
We don't want titles
Only, remove these bullets
And knives from our soft bodies
Let us lie safely
In our eternal home!

A Flying Angel

The child whose broken hands they tied
In a white gauze . . .
She urged her mother to tell her
Why her hands were tied like that
When the mother became confused
And couldn't find an answer,
She whispered to her: my little one, you became an angel.
Is it not true that angels have white wings?
The little one believed her mother
Slowly, she is recovering,
Moving her hands like wings
And trying to fly.

A Star

May be the child Chantal Awad was dreaming too much.
Dreaming to become a novelist or a great poet
Or a famous movie star
Yes, befitting her it was to be a movie star
With wide eyes and an angelic face
A long neck, a warm smile,
A hair dropping down to her shoulders,
A delicate sense, a sharp intellect
A complete intuition and a great name . . .
But, alas!
A booby-trapped car,
A car loaded in all types of death, killings, and destruction
Blew up her home and her mother
Blew up her tiny body and her small dream.
No camera
No pictures
No warm scenes to create a happy ending to the movie.
But slow down . . . slow down
Look up to the sky
Look up closely
Are you not seeing there at the top that she became a real
   star?
A star that sparkles with love, tenderness, beauty, and
   light?

*Chantal Awad died as a martyr with her mother from the blind
bombing at the Jermana neighbourhood in Damascus.

Infinite Innocence

The sad Aleppo man
Was sitting on a rubble
Which was caused by warplanes
Putting the milk bottle
Into his infant's mouth
(Maybe she was the only one who was left for him)
The infant was drinking her milk with infinite innocence
Raising one foot to the sky
As if she was telling them: all your frightening planes
Don't equal this little foot.

Mourning

*For the child who wore a red hair clip and kiwi color socks,
and was drowned in the Aegean Sea*

My child,
My sweet child,
We will soon escape the motherland's hell!
Come on, climb on the boat,
Climb on it quietly.
We will cross that beautiful blue sea.
We will reach the promised land,
The land of love and beauty,
The land of innocence, childhood, and happiness . . .!
You will go to school there
Without fear of killings and kidnappings.
You will have affectionate nannies,
Friends with golden hair.
You will play plenty.
You will sleep deeply,
Dreaming of colorful butterflies
And white flowers.
No escape . . . no escape
The boat sank to the bottom of the sea.
The dreams, hopes, and wishes staggered with it.
No escape for anybody, no escape for anything . . .
No escape . . .
Mourning
Mourning
Mourning . . .

The Child Who Was Orphaned

Raids after raids after raids . . .
The home transformed to heaps, dusts, and ruins.
The child who was orphaned sat
At the sidewalk, aligned exactly with her bedroom.
Opening her notebook,
She drew an enormous home
With large rooms, many windows, and tall doors;
She drew a spacious green garden
For her siblings to play within;
She walled the garden with flowers and trees.
Then she drew the sky in blue color
With birds flying instead of warplanes.
The home which the orphaned child drew
Became an orphan.

Shooting Down a Plane

The Aleppo child holds his plastic gun,
Standing by the window all day.
His mother insists that he close the window and sit down,
Fearing for him . . . because of snipers.
He says to her: no, mother!
I won't rest until I shoot down a plane.

The Pacifier

The infant Natalie Alkhateeb
Who had been martyred in the Horanian town Tafas . . .
Her family insisted on burying the pacifier with her
Because, if she cried, starved, or was frightened
Or felt worried and lonely,
Her guardian angel
Will put it in her small mouth,
Calming her to go to sleep with innocence and
Peace.

Imagination

The Syrian child is watching TV
He imagines the box is a cow
And its antenna is an elephant trunk.
He imagines the officer is "Tom"
And the soldier is "Jerry",
Fighting each other for a piece of cheese.
He imagines the plane is a kite
And the rockets are heaven's gifts.
He imagines the bullets are pencil tips
And bombs are fireworks, illuminating the festival's joy.
A plane, "Meg", is hovering over the city sky,
Emptying its lethal cargo everywhere.
The child is no longer imagining . . .
His soul now is soaring high,
Illuminating heaven's paths.

A Vacation . . .

At the refugee camp,
The Syrian child is asking his father disapprovingly:
Did you bring us to this place for a vacation?
Where is the sea?
Where are the children's swings?
Where are the kites?
Where are the colorful balloons?
Where are the ice cream and candy shacks?
The father lowers his head with grief and sorrow,
Mumbling: We didn't come here for a vacation, son!
But tomorrow, when the sound of guns pauses
And the roar of the planes stops,
I promise, we will return to our home
And we will go to the sea.
I will rent a beautiful camp near the beach.
You will swim and play and have fun with other children.
You will ride the swings, too.
You will send colorful balloons
And kites all the way to the sky.
I will buy you cold ice cream and delicious candy.
I will buy you everything, my son.
Everything!

Survival

The small child asks her mother,
Why are we leaving our home alone under the shelling?
With tears pouring down her face, the mother answers:
For you not to be left alone
Or for me not to be left alone
Or for both of us to survive, my child!

The Heart-Ball

The boy who lost his feet
From the random bombardment . . .
He was playing football with his peers.
They kicked the ball with their feet,
But he kicked it with his heart.

Utmost Innocence

When the men were occupied with lifting the bodies
And the rest of the alive ones from under the rubbles,
The small child was busy lifting his bicycle,
Mumbling some prayer that no harm came upon it.

Talbiseh's Children

In the early morning, they woke up
They dressed up in holiday clothes
They wore perfumes
They titivated themselves
They went to have fun and to play . . .
They found by accident a tank, resting
They said among themselves: what are we going to do with
    this savage beast?
Without much thinking,
They brought ropes,
Hanging it up from its neck
And swinging upon it happily.
With sadness, the tank said: when I was young,
I wanted to be a donkey, or a swing, or even a fly,
But they forced me, turning me into a ravenous
    mechanical beast.
Today, however, Talbiseh's children made my dream
    come true.
They turned me in to a swing.
They swayed on me like butterflies.
Oh, my returned childhood!
Oh, what an overwhelming happiness!

Al-Sham

The mother was telling her child,
One day, we will return to Al-Sham.
Al-Sham is so beautiful,
The most beautiful city in the universe, son.
When the mother had a new baby girl,
The child noticed a small mole (sham) on his sister's cheek.
He said to his mother while hugging her,
I love Sham so much.
Al-Sham is the most beautiful city in the universe, mother.
When are we going back to Al-Sham?

Raids

At the first raid, he lost his shoes
At the second raid, he lost his fingers
At the third raid, he lost his foot
At the fourth raid, he lost his leg
At the fifth raid, he didn't lose anything
He was walking with lightning feet
Together with his angel peers
Who preceded him to heaven.

Deraa's Children

Remember when you pass by Deraa
That its children have fingers made of gold.

In February of 2011, Deraa's children wrote slogans
    on walls,
Demanding freedom and overthrowing the regime,
Which provoked the tyrant authority in the city.
So, they proceeded to arrest the children
And plunged them in to prisons.
They also preformed upon them
The ultimate types of tortures, and postponed
Releasing them, which enraged and angered
The town people.
So, from there, the Syrian revolution's spark was lit up.

Remember when you pass by Deraa
To present its children with chalks
In rainbow colors,
Telling them that their fingers
Are still made of gold.

Noticing Our Death!

My father fled.
My mother fled.
My brothers and sisters fled.
We all fled from death, manslaughter,
And destruction's hell.
But when we heard that things
Calmed down a little,
We packed our bags.
We all wanted to go back home.
My father palpated his heartbeat.
He listened to his breath.
He placed his hand on his heart.
He tried to move his body.
Everything in him was
Extinct, static, motionless.
Everything in us, too, was
Extinct, static, motionless.
Suddenly, we noticed
That we were killed elsewhere!

The Tale about the Girl
Who Went to the Store

I missed my school so much.
I told my mother, I will go to the nearby store
To buy a pencil, notebook and an eraser.
On the street, I was happy mumbling a song.
Suddenly, I saw my blood drops
Pouring to the ground.
I felt my head.
I found a bullet settled in it!
I remembered the sniper's face
Who was on the top of the building,
Laughing his yellow laugh at my face.
My mother regretted letting me go alone.
She cried so much.
My father cried.
My brother cried.
My doll cried.
I stretched my hands from heaven,
Wiping the tears off from their swollen eyes
And comforting their sorrowful hearts.

The Child, Fatima Al-Meglaj

I was a child.
I had a head graced with long hair,
Combed by my mother every day.
My father was saying whenever he saw me:
How beautiful is your hair, my child!
I was smiling at him, shaking my head approvingly.
Today, I looked at the mirror and couldn't find it!
Immediately, I remembered my assassin.
He had a ghoul's head and a flying monster's body.
He didn't give me a chance to breathe or utter a word.
Suddenly, he cut off my head,
Severing it from my body.
I shivered from pain.
My blood poured hot and warm on to the tiles.
I saw my soul hugging my families' souls
That preceded me to heaven.
My neighbour who carried me headless said:
The world after you, my little one,
Will be forever headless.
Because I was small and with no head,
I didn't understand the significance of his statement.

*Fatima Al-Meglaj: the child whose body was found with no head
at the Kufer Ouid village in the city of Edlib had been exposed to
a brutal massacre, and the Al-Meglaj family was one of its victims.

They Were Our Children, and They Became Your Angels

Those children
Will not carry their bags after today
Will not go to their schools
Will not read or learn
Will not write or paint
Will not run or rejoice
Will not fill the yard with plays, noises, and life!
O God, those children were our children,
Our hearts that were walking on earth
Now they became your angels,
Your hearts that fly in heaven.
So, do not let them wonder, suffer, and get tired
Between stars, planets, and moons.
Do not let them sleep without warm and clean beds.
O God, do not let them die twice!

A Child Looking for His Father

Near the building's debris,
A small child carries
A small stone.
Placing it in the big stone's lap,
He whispers to it: here, I found your father!
Now, I am going to find my father too.
He walks on with the men,
Searching vigorously through the rubbles.

The Structure

The planes bombed
His school and his home,
And his small room that was filled with toys.
In great enthusiasm,
The small child started
Building from the scattered debris
His school and his home,
And his room that was filled with toys.
Now, he is learning how to read and write
As if he were in school;
Wandering and rejoicing as if he were in his home;
Sleeping, waking up and playing
As if he were in his room that was filled with toys!

Adel, My Beautiful Child!

Adel, my beautiful child,
Who asked you to leave home?
Who asked you to go to church?
Who asked you to go pray and celebrate
And to participate in raising the cross?
Is it not your mother who said to you that day:
"Children's heaven is their homes,
And death's hell is lurking around them, if they left?"
Did you not know that the sniper's heart is blind
And his bullets penetrate the bodies of the innocent?
Did you not know that this day you will be his?
Adel, my beautiful child, my small child,
Oh, I wish you got sick that day and stayed home!
Oh, I wish you disappointed the sniper's aim and
His bullets' lust!
Oh, I wish . . .
Goodbye, my little child.
Goodbye, my beautiful child.
Goodbye . . .
Now, I am hearing your sweet cooing
That comes from the heaven's midst.
Amid condolences,
I am trying to be comforted . . .

*Adel Zaatery was martyred by a sniper's bullets on the way back from church after celebrating the cross holiday in Haresta.

Sipan* Asks Me . . .

In Kurdish, in a voice tinged with sorrow,
Sipan asks me:
"Father, why are they killing children in Syria?"
Because . . .
My voice trembles
And I can't hold back my tears.
I hide my face from him,
Run to the next room,
And cry silently
As mothers do.

*Sipan is the name of the poet's son.

I Was a Fetus,
and I Didn't Have a Name Yet!

I was a fetus, and I didn't have a name yet.
The plane dropped a large bomb over our home.
It slashed my mother's belly into two pieces.
I was happy to step out early
From the dark womb to the light of life!
But I was too small,
As tender as butterflies.
My body couldn't endure the bright light,
And with the fragments that settled in it,
I died instantly.
I was buried with my mother.
Without a name, I remained forever.
But what really confuses me . . .
In what name will God call me?
And if He calls me with a name,
How may I know that it is my name
And it is me He meant exactly?

Father, Don't Leave Me Alone!

Father, o father,
Don't leave me alone, orphaned, fractured . . .
Don't let my tears pour down grieving for you!
Did you not tell me, o father: I always want you
To be happy, son?
Did you not tell me, o father: I don't want to see tears
In your eyes as long as I live?
Father, o father,
Don't leave me alone, orphaned, fractured . . .
To whom shall I say,
Hug me close to your heart,
Kiss me,
Hold me tight,
Coddle me
Tickle me,
Play with me?
To whom shall I say all of that, o father, to whom?
Father, o father,
Don't leave me alone, orphaned, fractured . . .
In the cold winter nights, who will put a cover on me?
Who will wake me up, prepare breakfast, and take me
To school?
Who will teach me, and help me with my difficult
Homework?
Who, o father, who?
Father, o father,
Don't leave me alone, orphaned, fractured . . .
Who will be beside me if I trip and fall?
Who will touch my hair when I am tired?
Who will warm me up when I am cold?
Who will be concerned when I am sick?
Who will comfort me when I am sad?

Who, o father, who?
Don't leave me alone, orphaned, fractured . . .
Who will buy me toys?
Who will celebrate my birthday?
Who will present me with beautiful gifts?
Who will buy me new cloths?
To whom shall I say, thank you from my heart,
I love you, father?
To whom shall I say that, to whom?
Goodbye, my father.
Goodbye, my kind, fabulous, affectionate father . . .
Goodbye.

In Lamentation of Beautiful Homes

A small Syrian princess talks about their journey after their homes were bombed and turned into rubbles and debris.

The first child says:
Our home was spacious and beautiful
With five rooms and a guest hall
And a special corner for dining
But now, it turned into a compassionate shade tree
And our kitchen became the outdoors stones.

The second child says:
Our home was very, very high
On the sixth floor of a building
Overlooking the main street
Hugging the city from all sides
But now, it turned into a tent in exile
And the brothers – as my father says –
Save us even from air.

The third child says:
Our home was capacious with many windows
And a porch filled with roses, basil, and jasmine pots
But now, it became a school with thousands of refugees
No sheets, no pillows, no covers, no white beds.

The fourth child says:
Our home was vast
A water fountain was in its midst, with bees buzzing
And birds chirping
Through its bubble
Smelling the laurel . . .
But now, we don't have a home or a shelter
We became nomads, moving from house to house,
Received by the hearts of good people.

The fifth child says:
Our home was in the village
A vast garden stood in front of it
An orchard like heaven at its back
We used to pick fruit from it
And plant all kind of vegetables in it
But now, it became a dark cave,
Filled with rats, roaches, and insects.

The sixth child says:
Our home was like a palace
Decorated with antiques, paintings, and chandeliers
I was there like a small, pampered princess
Listening in long nights to grandmother's tales
But now, it became shadows of dilapidated buildings,
And walls are sheltering us from the planes' bombardment.

A School

A school . . .

Its walls completely pierced

Traces of spilled blood on the seats

Crushed chalks

And childish scribbles filling the green board:

"Freedom . . . The people want to overthrow the regime . . .

The sun shines . . . Father and mother . . ."

A chair and a cane . . .

Fragments and so many bullets . . .

The students . . .

In the cemetery!

Alive and Well, with Their Lord

The girl: if I get killed,
I want to become a mockingbird, building my nest in our
    home's cavities
To be close to my family and my friend, the neighbour's
    daughter.
The boy: I want to become a nightingale, leaping from
    tree to tree
Singing to my mother the sweetest and the most beautiful
    tunes.
The girl: if I get killed,
I want to become a violet in our garden,
        perfuming the space, wishing my mother will pick me
        and put me close to her silky beautiful long hair
The boy: I want to become rain,
        falling on the trees my father planted
        to ease his pain and to cheer up his sad heart a little . . .
The girl: but I want to stay alive
The boy: me too, I want to stay alive
The girl and the boy
The father and the mother
The brothers and sisters . . .
They are now all
"Alive and well, with their Lord."

Surviving Miraculously

I was too small.
I didn't understand what was going on around me.
My only concern in life was the milk bottle
And the affectionate touch of my mother's hand.
The adults were talking with worry
About planes and bombardments.
I didn't understand what they meant,
But I flinched from time to time
From its strange sound.
Today, they bombed our home.
I found myself between the rubbles.
My face and body were covered in dust.
I was very frightened.
I cried, screamed, and called for help
Until they lifted me up.
I miraculously survived.
My mother kissed my left cheek,
My father kissed the right.
I felt fine,
But I was very tired.
I dozed off on my father's forearm.
Immediately, I had a dream of the milk bottle
And of that affectionate touch of my mother's hand.

Hunger

The infant who survived death
Miraculously . . .
They pulled him out from under the rubbles
He was calm and quiet
Nothing concerned him
Only, he was so hungry
That he kept sucking at his finger greedily.

Tearful Eyes

With her tearful eyes, a young girl says:
We had a home
We had an address
We had a neighbourhood
We had friends and neighbours
No homes, no address
No neighbourhood, no friends, no neighbours!

An Entertaining Game

A damaged tank . . .
The children converted it to an entertaining game
Once, they climbed on it and slid down
Once, they swung on its long neck
Once, they descended to its belly, tampering
    with its buttons
Once, they stretched on its back
Once, they screamed into its nozzle
Once, they jumped from above it
Once, they hid underneath it
Once, they kicked its behind
And when they got totally bored from it,
They urinated on it
And then, they went home happy.

A Meeting in Heaven

In heaven,
Five Syrian children met
The first was from Al-Hula
The second was from Daria
The third was from Helfaya
The fourth was from Sare Kaniye
The fifth was from Talbeseh
The first one said: Helfaya, o my love
The second one said: Daria, o Daria
The third one said: Helfaya, o my bread
The fourth one said: Sare Kaniye, o my spring
The fifth one said: Talbeseh, o my land
Heaven said: Syria, o my Mother.

The Child Who Lost Everything

Where is my foot?
I want to run after the birds.
Where is my hand?
I want to clap for the butterflies.
Where is my brother?
I want to play with him.
Where is my sister?
I want to tease her.
Where is my father?
I want to accompany him to the market.
Where is my mother?
I want to sit on her warm lap.
Where are my friends?
I want to go to school with them.
The confused child
Lost in the planes' bombardment
His brother, sister, father, mother, and half of his body
Now, he is lying in the field hospital
Running in his dream after the birds
Clapping for the butterflies
Playing with his brother
Teasing his sister
Accompanying his father to the market
Sitting on his mother's lap
And going to school with his friends.

Inspection

1

After each bombardment,
The Syrian mother runs fast
To inspect her children.
After each news bulletin,
I run fast to inspect my children!

2

After each bombardment,
The Syrian mother runs fast
To inspect her children.
After each news bulletin,
My children run fast
To inspect me!

Pink Panther

Once upon a time,
Syrian children
Imagined the president as Pink Panther
Who eliminates the enemies one by one
And fulfills the rosy dreams for children
    and their homeland!
Now, in reality, Syrian children realize
That the president became a savage killer,
Devouring the children one by one,
Creating destruction, terror and nightmares
For them and for their homeland.

*The Pink Panther in this context is the same as the humor-filled, likable cartoon character famous among children in many countries.

A Very Sad Syrian Tale

Once upon a time,
There was a bloody terrifying ruler in Syria.
He inherited the reign from his tyrant father!
He was ordering his soldiers
To severe children's heads from their bodies,
To crush their skulls with axes and hammers,
To slit their throats with daggers and knives,
To cut open their bellies with swords and spears,
To remove their nails and gouge their eyes,
To smash their fingers, hands, and legs,
To cut off their genitals,
To pour fire and lead on their tiny bodies,
To cut them off from water, milk, and medicine . . .
The tale said that the ruler was proud of his murderous
    soldiers, "The Homeland Protectors",
Attributing to them the utmost finest descriptions and titles.
The tale also said that from time to time
He stood at his palace's porch
That overlooked the districts of Damascus,
Cheerful,
Delighted,
Whispering quietly:
What harm would it do, if no child survived in this country
Other than two beautiful children, my two spoiled children?

*The Homeland Protectors: a title for the Syrian Arab army which
is now killing the country's people.

Sipan, My Little Child

Soon, my little child Sipan
Will come back from school.
So, I will be preparing food for him.
Yesterday, he told his sister
That he is going to write a poem about the Syrian children.
I don't know if he really wrote it,
Or just had a dream about it,
Or postponed it for some reason.
Anyway,
I won't ask him
If he wrote it or not.

A Dialogue Between a Father and a Son

1

Where are you, father?
At autumn's age, son.
What are you doing there, father?
I am waiting for an orange wagon
To collect my yellow leaves, son.

2

Where are you, father?
At the age of eight, son.
What are you doing there, father?
Remembering myself when I was your age, son.

3

Where are you, father?
At the old age, son.
What are you doing there, father?
Counting what is left of life's grains, son.

4

Do you love me, father?
How could I not, son?
How much do you love me, father?
As much as the extent of innocence in your heart, son!

5

What are you thinking about, father?
Of things that make us think, son.
What things make us think, father?
The devastation of human beings and their brutalities, son.

6

Why you are sad, father?
For my existence, son.
Why you are happy, father?
Because of your existence, son!

7

Do you love the sun, father?
Only when it plays with you, son!
And what else, father?
When you draw it, son!

8

What worries you, father?
Nothing, my son!
But you are saturated with pain, father.
Don't worry, son!
I am only training my heart how to stare.

9

Why are you tired, father?
I am not tired, son.
But you are distracted from life, father.
No son, the life had been distracted away from me.

10

Why is the earth so vast, father?
So that people can live and wander in it, son.
But why they are fighting for it, father?
Because that is their nature, son.

11

Why are you in pain, father?
Because I have a headache, son.
Why do you have a headache, father?
Do not bother son!
It is something inherited from grandfathers and fathers.
Am I going to inherit it from you, father?
No son, you won't inherit it from me
Because it stopped at me,
And I became the end of the suffering, son!

In a Coma

On May 13, 2020, I had an operation to have a kidney stone removed. As a result of a medical error during anesthesia, I fell into a full coma for two consecutive days. I miraculously survived death. After I left the intensive care unit on the fourth day, I frantically wrote this text in Kurdish as if I was in a race against time.

In a coma,
Your body is not yours
Your mind is not yours
Your brain is not yours
Your soul is not yours
Your being is not yours
Your dreams are not yours
Absolutely nothing is yours!
You are just a vulnerable bird,
Stumbling in his flight, like a blind who lost his cane
In a fierce war against blindness.

In a coma,
You don't know your name or your title
You don't know your birth date or your age
You don't know what time you are in or what day
You don't know what month, what season
What year, what century you are in
Nothing has value in your eternally vast passivity.

In a coma,
You don't feel the time!
No value for time nor for the clock
No value for the sunrise nor the sunset
No value for morning nor night
No value for light nor darkness
No value for fertility nor drought
No value for trees nor flowers
No value for a butterfly's tenderness nor a bird's flutter

No value for the clouds nor the blue sky . . .
In a coma, you are present
And your real presence is your absence
And getting lost in the abyss of nothingness
Without limbs nor legs nor strong feet!

In a coma,
You forget every day's walking paths
Forget the road to the coffee shop
Forget the road to the bar
Forget the road to the workplace
Forget the road to the house
Forget your keychain
Forget your keys
Forget your door's lock
Forget your library
Forget the smell of your books
Forget your notebooks and pens
Forget your poems
Forget your daily rituals
Forget your hat
Forget your coat
Forget your shirt
Forget if you are dressed or naked
No difference!
Forgetting is the mystery of a coma and its blessing.

In a coma,
Nothing has value but the oxygen tube which pumps air
    to your lungs
And to the hoses which feed your body with medicines
And to the anesthetics that sedate the already sedated
No value but for the adhesive tapes on your chest which
    measure your unfelt heartbeats.
No value but for the bed which they throw you into,
    motionless.
Nothing indicates that you breathe.
Nothing indicates that you exist in existence.

In a coma,
You won't feel pain even if it's severe
You won't fight your breath even if it's a strong rattle
You won't cry even if there is an obligatory reason to cry
You won't love, and you won't know why you won't
You won't cry, and you won't know why you won't
No astonishment
No outbursts
No amazement . . .
You look like a statue, sculpted from boredom,
Or an invisible icon in an abandoned church.

In a coma,
You are like those monkeys
That don't see
Don't hear
Don't talk
And don't understand their surroundings
Although
They remain real beings of flesh, blood and tears.

In a coma,
Your eyelids won't flutter
Your cheeks won't blush
Your forehead won't lift up
Your eyelashes won't blink
Your heart won't beat
You won't notice the sweat drop on your forehead
You won't wipe the black blood stain from your neck
You will just fade away; your capabilities will vanish and
    they will become less than an ash and lighter than dust.

Coma is a trick
A plot
A cave
A trap
Beware you don't get stuck between its sharp teeth
And its fierce claws

Coma is stupidity!
How foolish your intention looks
When you attempt to step on its thresholds,
Trying to enter its vestibule
And its dark terrifying corridors.

In a coma,
Between alertness and absence,
You will probably speak as a great philosopher
Not like any other philosopher
Neither before nor after . . .
Wisdom after wisdom will come out
From your heavy tongue
And your hoarse throat
And your wounded pronunciation,
And your sore lips.

In a coma,
You are dead.
Yes, you are dead!
No one can wake you up
And give your body and soul their life back,
Except your lover's tender hand
And her heart's infinite music.
So, listen!
So, listen!
Listen with all your senses
And with all the remaining breath in your chest.
Then slowly, slowly you will open your eyes
And inevitably, you will wake up from your stupid coma.

16-17/5/2020
University Hospital in Bonn, Germany

Da Nany . . . Da Nany*
(De nenî . . . De nenî)

My eyes were staring at the far horizon,
Choosing a star or two for you.
The angels from above knew that you are coming, blessed
With God's light, calm like his secluded corners.
They were patting my shoulder
With compassion and confidence,
And saying to me: a little patience, a little composure . . .
Hewa will arrive soon, wreathed with lights.

So, you came, my daughter.
You came to rob the sun its golden tiara tomorrow,
To ignite a lantern from its lashes for our future days.
You came to be the home poem, and the painting
For our quiet life.
You came to smooth out with your impish iron
The wrinkles of the heart's sheet.
You came to close the distance between me and me.
You came.
You are welcome, welcome.

Tomorrow,
I will draw your smile with an eye's brush.
I will guard you with the vigilante soul's lilies.
I will crown you an angel in the mirror.
I will spray you with perfume,
And with quince water, I will wash your feet!

Daughter,
I will buy you a small journal, and you will scribe in it
The buds of your heart and the iris of your dreams,
And I will record in it the stuttering of your words.
I will stay up by you, rocking you with warmth
And tenderness.
I will sing you lullabies.

Da nany
Da nany
Da nany
Until you fall asleep.

My child,
My little one,
My love,
I will put you on my shoulders and teach you
The language of trees!
I will listen to you.
I will listen to your early query
And your small letters that look like a bird's mouth.
I will take care of you as I take care of the flowers of love.
I will plant you in the word's vessels
And cover you with the petals of poems.

My daughter,
My child,
My little one,
My friend, welcome!
Welcome,
Welcome in the eye, the soul and the heartbeats.
Welcome . . .

*Da Nany . . . Da Nany is a lullaby that Kurdish mothers sing by
their child's cradle; it speaks of warmth, sorrow, and compassion.

My Children's Dreams

My son says: I like the graceful deer.
I tell him: When you grow up, one of them will charm you,
And I would have you marry her.
Here he is, dancing with joy and humming a song:
When I grow up, my father would have me marry
A graceful deer, and I will love her,
I will love her my entire life.

My daughter says: I like the wobbling swans in the lake!
I tell her: When you grow up, I will buy you a white dress
And send you with the swans to the other side of the bank.
You will find a handsome groom waiting for you there.
Here she is, dancing with joy and humming a song:
When I grow up, my father will buy me a white dress.
I will be a swan, and I will find my groom
On the other side of the bank.
Definitely, I will find him,
And I will love him my entire life.

My Son Asks

My small child is standing on the beach.
He looks amazed at the sea.
With complete innocence, he asks me:
Father, how many barrels of water is the sea?
Smiling, I shift the question back to him:
How many do you estimate it to be?
He says: twenty barrels!
Jokingly, I say: it's fewer than twenty barrels.
Laughing,
Laughing,
Laughing . . .
And he says: how foolish you are, father!
All this water, and you estimate it to be
Fewer than twenty barrels?!

Sleeping Calmly

In the forest, the bad wolf met with a girl in a red hood.

The wolf tricked her and delayed her arrival

To her grandmother's cottage in the forest.

Then he went to the cottage,

Ate the grandmother, and disguised in her clothes.

When the girl in the red hood arrived, he ate her too.

Isn't it strange listening to this very scary story?

My children sleep with utmost innocence,

And complete calm . . .

Beware, Child!

Beware, child!
Don't bend over too much,
You will fall from the high rock.
Don't go to that abandoned place,
The snake will bite you.
Don't run toward the railroad,
The train will hit you.
Don't run after it.
It's not a kite.
It's not for children!
No!
No!
Beware, and don't be fooled!
Stay where you are, child.
Don't get out of the painting.
If you get out, the colors shall melt
And splatter here and there,
And the painter's heart will break from sorrow.
So, stay where you are child,
Stay . . .

Sipan

My head hurts.

No aspirin at home, nor any sedative to lessen my pain . . .

At this moment,

Exactly at this moment,

I want for Sipan to come

And knock with his soft hands my heart's door

So that I say to him: thank you my son, thank you!

My head no longer hurts.

Translations by

Sinan Anton

A Rose for the Heart of Life

Tomorrow, You Will Be an Old Man
(For me, in a quarter of a century, more or less)

Tomorrow, you will be an old man
The cane, always with you
You will walk alone
You will mutter to yourself like all old geezers do
You will become obstinate, hard of hearing, and slow
You will ask for help when you need it
But no one will respond
You will dream of the past
And the good old days
While your grandson will think of the future
And days to come
You will curse this vapid generation
Repeating itself like a broken record
How wonderful our generation was!
You will be the butt of jokes in the family
They will laugh at you and your positions
Which you think are right on
Your lips will let out a sarcastic smile
Whenever they mention words like "stubbornness",
"Vigor", and "faith in the future"
You might even laugh
Your bones will soften
Illnesses will roam freely in your body
Without permission
All your desires will be extinguished,
Except the desire to die
There will be no friend or a companion
Loneliness will be your support and comrade

You will always be ready to depart
The threshold of the grave will entice you
And keep you company

All the angels will betray you and leave
Only Azrael will approach you as a last friend
Perhaps you will say just as you are about to go:
If I die burry me here in the strangers' cemetery
Perhaps these words
Will be you your final wish.

Beethoven and the Kurds

I look at Beethoven's sculpture.
He appears sad.
Crowds of Kurds
Inspect the city center with their steps.
Nothing dwells in them except a longing.
Beethoven cries.

I look at the Rhine
Cleaving the city into two.
It appears sad.
Is it sad for the Euphrates?
The Euphrates is sad.

My Mother's Chants

1. The Vision Chant

This morning, my mother was sitting alone at home
Mending my brother Mahmoud's pants
Torn by yesterday's mischief
The needle pierced her finger and warm blood flowed on
    the thread
The pants were stained and my mother's thoughts were
    muddled
She swore to my father and the neighbors
That she saw me or my shadow
Or saw me without my shadow passing before her this
    morning
And when she saw me,
She was so eager; she was confused and was about to
    hug me
But the needle betrayed her and pierced her finger
Was I really there
Or was it my mother's heart?

2. The Longing Chant

Mother,
Thirty years . . . and I am still running with a barefoot heart
Whenever I see a woman wearing a long dress
Or a white scarf on her head
I call out to her: mother, mother
Mother!
Thirty years and six thousand miles
Exiled from roses, the sunrise and the face of angels,
Mother's face
Thirty years . . .

Whenever I write about a woman
Whenever I draw a woman
I find myself writing about my mother
Clothing the image with my mother's colors
Thirty shrouds, thirty graves, thirty . . .
I am filled with hope and peace of mind
Whenever I lay my head
On my mother's chest

3. The Passion Chant

The inscriptions on the walls of our mud house
The yellow paint on the door
The family picture, carefully hung next to Imam Ali's
The traces of a tattoo on the baking tin
The big quiet stone next to the door,
Always ready to receive guests
Shelves crowded with old newspapers
The lamp, philosophizing with a long luminous tongue
The hanging mat, always ready for prayer
The sacred laugh that brought all this passion
And this weariness
Is my mother's laugh.

In Praise of My Father

My father, his trousers flowing
His shirt adorned with the scent of earth
His forehead, wide as a field of wheat,
Is still gazing with eyes of love and longing
For the green olive trees
Measuring with the sugar of yearning
The distance between Shiye and Bonn
Whose name he knows by heart

He is still surging
Like the river Afrin
Hard, stubborn, and rough
He only fears God
And separation
From another son

He is still repeating his supplications
In his broken Arabic
On the prayer beads
Five times every day
Asking God a thousand times
Between one bow and another
To protect his children from harm

He is still simple
Bowing to guests
Prayer
And the seedlings in his little orchard
But nothing else

He is still sitting
On his wooden chair
In the courtyard

Speaking to his guests with pride
Listening with pride
Silent with pride
Laughing with pride
Shaking hands with the vast distances
In the horizon
With pride

He is still comparing
Butterflies and humans
Trees and humans
Love and humans
The sun and humans
Earth and humans

. . .

But when he listens
To the news every day
On his old radio
Which never leaves his side
Wrinkles and decades of sorrow
Invade his facial features
Yet he mutters:
Humans are still so beautiful!

Translations by

Azad Akkash

Hussein Habasch

A Wound Called AFRIN

I shall restore my heart
from the devastation it received through the years.
I shall remove the dark stains of sadness,
the blue bruises of pain.
From its walls, I shall remove the dry crusts
and the deep wrinkles that appeared on its skin.
I shall remove the decaying flesh,
the fat built-up in its arteries.
Yet, I am keeping a single deep wound
that keeps growing in my heart,
a wound called Afrin!
I shall never let anybody mess with it,
to come close to it,
or to try to heal it.
It is the wound of my heart alone.
With it, my heart beats get regulated.
For its sake, my heart lives.

*Afrin is the name of the poet's city of birth.

Every Day

Every day,
I pass by the madhouse.
From the third-floor's window,
A woman shows up.
She cries: Help, I need help!
I say to her: I need that also!
She raises a wry laugh
And asks me: Are you mad like me?
In all seriousness, I answer: Yes, sure.
She shakes her head and says:
Then we will prevail!
To her, I raise the sign of victory
That is going to be lost anyway,
And I move on.

A Traveler

I

As his puzzled legs like, he travels.
He crosses long distances and dangerous bridges
with no doubt that he will make it even over his dead body.
From springs, he drinks; in deep rivers, he swims.
He suckles fresh milk from the breasts of she-wolves:
"Thank you, fierce mothers," he says.
Under a plane tree, he rests, and with a provocative desire,
he contemplates the cracks in the valleys.
After a scared rabbit, he runs, and calms her with a carrot
that emerges from his heart like an arrow.
He wallows in grass and mimics the birds in the sky.
He jests with the squirrels, tossing them hazelnut;
here and there, he joins their jumps.
He waters a flower and in return, receives a whiff of
perfume as he whispers to her: "He who has flowers, has no
need for God."
When he feels hungry, he knocks on doors like a passerby,
asking for bread to share with his siblings, the birds.
He falls in love with the first woman he meets, as if
she's been his woman for a millennium;
he leaves a kiss on her forehead.
He does not care when his heart is worn out of love or vice,
and he says to it: "Thank you, my big heart!"
Near a sparkling spring water, he lies down into a sleep of
all nightmares. He opens his eyes to the sudden appearance
of a lioness nearby.
In a cold manner, he says to her: "Claw's morning,
lioness!" He asks indifferently:
"Do you prey on dreadful poets?"
The lioness turns her face and runs away from him.
He tightens his backpack, and off he goes toward oddity,
with no burden of a home, a homeland, a woman or a child.

Wherever he stops at and fills the place with the water of
temptation, he calls it homeland.
Wherever he takes the earth as a bed and gets drunk on the
damp grass, he calls it home.
Each woman he comes across in his travels,
he calls his own.
A sparrow, a butterfly or a star . . . let his child be.
Here he is standing on a highland, getting his act together
and kicking the butt of sorrow.
As intense as his own death, he shouts: "Oh life, I will
devour you! Where to run?"

II

He left no sea without slating his body with, nor a mountain
without giving it a pat on the head.
No forest, unless he obtained it out of its arcane; no land,
unless he planted it with his madness.
No language, unless he learned its most impudent
vocabulary, most hurtful and evil.
He passes through each and every border; "Thank you, my
strong legs," he says.
He finds himself everywhere, "thank you, my wanderer
soul that roams the world."
In the huts of the poor, he lived; he became one of them.
Into the palace of the rich, he entered; he could not stand it.
He knew hotels, bars and sidewalks the same way he knew
his parents, siblings and friends.
To homelessness, the same way as to his torn socks . . .
He drank, got drunk, smoked. With indiscretion, with
delirium, he filled the world.
He loved trees more than human beings, birds more than
planes, autumn more than the other seasons.
He loved the night, he grasped his hand and told him: "You
blind man, how much you enlighten the hearts of poets."

He knew the cold and wrapped himself in it. He tested the
strong accent of the snow, he cared not for it!
He did not take storms in earnest; his face kept butting
against the forehead of the wind.
As he dies in the grave where he lies, there will be no ease;
from one grave to another, one graveyard to another . . .
He comes across the ancient dead men; hears the bones
rattling across the fresh dead to hear them decay.
Across those who were sentenced to death, to bliss, and
those who are swinging on the Straight Path.
The one eternal traveler he is; one doesn't dare to ask: why
do you not rest?
God shall judge him, yet "What has the insanely sad one
done to be judged", the traveler shall ask.
"Why did you create me after the image of the mad and not
after the pure image of yours?"
He attacked frustration, but it penetrated him with a bullet
that was not stray.
He hit the roads until they were worn out, the soles of his
feet cracked, one by one, the toes fell apart. "It's all right,
travelling is prettier."
In his entire life, he had no money; scraps were enough
for him.
On the edge of an abyss, his life was. On the sharp edge of
existence, his heart was.
With stubbornness, he kept telling life: "Be generous with
me, o life! With growing intensity, be generous with me;
for I love you with all of my passion and immense
generosity."

III

As a guest at the garden of the blind,
he came so close, staring at their eyes,
beaming with blindness.

All of a sudden, he remembered J. L. Borges, "If I could
live again my life, . . . I'll try to make more mistakes."
He remembered the blind man of Ma`arat al-Nu`man,
healing pain with forgiveness, forgiving no one.
He remembered José Saramago leading the blind all over
the city, killing and wreaking havoc . . .
He remembered the lover of Jun'ichirō Tanizaki, piercing
his eyes to be as blind as his beloved.
He remembered the old blind man of his village reciting
from the book of God and gathering the angels around,
and how, he himself, was gathering all the devils around
old blind men.
Now, he opens his heart, totally blind . . . from the abyssal
depths of his blindness, he beams with ecstasy.

IV

Rain is tapping against the pane of his heart.
He sticks his head out and says: You rain, hit it here
on my head,
exactly on the carefully polished skull.
I want the rotten mind and his resident farce
to be driven away!
Under the strong, your strong stings; I want the salt of
wisdom and the pus of certitude to dissolve.
I want the rock of quietude to crumble, the throne of the
taboos to collapse.
I want to keep the madness glittering, beaming, enchanting,
bizarre and out of norm.
I want the beings to breathe sharply in amazement and
repeat: "How majestic is this enormous mad traveler!"

The Difference Between You and Me

The difference between you and me
Is that you sit cross-legged,
Leisurely savoring your glass of wine
While I wrap myself around myself
As I gulp from the glass of pain at the hospital.
You post the photo of your ninety something mother on
Facebook, still in her prime.
And I remember the complexions of my seventy something
Mother with all her wrinkles.
You see her every day and place a peck on her cheeks,
Whereas I have seen her only twice in twenty-two years.
I kiss her photo every day in longing.
God bless our mothers!
You follow all football matches.
You laugh, comment, cheer and support this team
Against that one
While I follow all the agonies of my people in Afrin.
I weep, despond, curse and grieve
For what has befallen them.
Your sister has a splendid house in the city center
Whilst my two sisters are vagrants, homeless
And vagabonds,
A family from Ghouta occupied the house of one,
And a family from Qalamun occupied the house
Of the other.
You sit with your only brother
And debate how to split your father's vast legacy
While I worry about the affairs of my brothers, exiled and
Fleeing, scattered around the globe.
I have no means to reunite them and to bring them
To safety.
Your country is Germany.

My country is Kurdistan.
Two worlds apart . . .
Germany is flourishing and growing
At each moment and every minute
While Kurdistan is slaughtered and murdered
At each moment and every second.
Your country is exporting Leopard tanks to kill what breath
Was left in the lungs of my country!
And my compatriots who miraculously survived
The killing machine
Are applying in scores for asylum in your country.
You were born with a golden spoon in your mouth,
And I was born with a poisonous challis in my mouth.
This is only a drop of an ocean of differences
Between you and me.
I shall not go on unfolding the pain that adjoined me
As a twin since birth.
Despite the differences you see between us,
I fully understand why you celebrate life.
I never understand why I despair over it!

A Kurd Would Love His Stubbornness!

I love these rugged mountains
and these slender rivers
with wobbly knees pouring into their charnel house.
I love these stones that defy sunrays
in the midsummer heat
and the frosty cold in midwinter chills.
I love this soil that resembles my body
and this land that foremost means the heart.
I love this dust, a coal for my eyes it is,
and this air, a balm for my lungs it is.
I love this skimpy terebinth
and the fragrant hawthorn.
I love cacti and its thorns,
olives and its yearnings.
I love this thin reed that serenades all the time
on the river bank,
this dark swamp where frogs continuously croak.
I love the daisy flower that resembles the whiteness
of my heart,
and these tulips that fraternize with my blood.
I love these mud houses
and these tents, fluttering on the outskirts of
forgotten villages.
I love this generous vine, the bequeather of grapes
and wine.
I love these yellow grain spikes, the bequeather of food
and bread.
I love these swaggering kite birds,
and these cicadas, continuously singing.
I love my land
from top to bottom
and from bottom to top,
just as a Kurd would love his stubbornness!

The Most Beautiful Side

Go neither to this side nor to that
Just stay where you are
Contemplate deeply
You will realize that all sides
Are almost enclosed
The most beautiful one
Is the side of your soul.

The Loner

I am a loner.
I am doing my best
So that I remain a loner.
But for God's sake,
What shall I do with my neighbour?
By going back and forth on the balcony,
She upsets the mood of my loneliness.

Sculptures

If the worst of the coronavirus crisis comes to pass,
The first thing to do is to make many sculptures
Of the toilet paper.
We will set them up
In the centers of major cities
By the entrances of train stations
And in front of the headquarters of the ministers
And the governments.
Without hesitation, we will be making them.
How valuable this precious paper is,
We did not know.
Oh, how ignorant we are!
We were not paying any attention to it in the past.
Oh, what a shame!
Then we are going to atone for our sins.
We will install many sculptures to befit its stature.
Lofty sculptures,
Standing tall,
Mighty,
White . . .
Will manifest
Motivation for the imagination,
And attract attention from all over!

I Want to Travel to Tirana

I want to travel to Tirana,
the magical city that has been blazing in my imagination
for thirty years.
I have not delighted myself in seeing her yet!
I want to go there to follow the traces
of that marvelous poet whom I came across by chance
in a fast train forty dreams ago,
from now and fifty pains in the heart since then!
I want to stroll in the parks where she strolls,
walk down in the streets where she walks,
sit in the coffee shops where she sits,
and get drunk in the bars where she does so.
I want to know the markets where she wanders,
the shops she buys from,
the clubs where she works out,
the libraries where she reads.
I want to get to know the routes to her house,
the trees that cast their shadow on her alley,
the fence that encloses her garden,
and the flowers that lead me to the traces of her footsteps.
I want to enter her house that I drew in my imagination,
stone after stone and corner after corner.
I want to come in from everywhere!
Through the walls, as swiftly as a magician who wants to
lay his destiny in the palms of her hands; from the ceiling,
with the mind's image of an angel that descended
from the sky, intending to grant her with a moon or a star;
from the chimney like a sparrow that shivers from the cold
and demands the warmth of her coat;
from the door like a man who seeks her acceptance;
through the window like a rainy cloud that intends to make
her hair wet; through the balcony like the smell of basil,

intending to perfume her mirror, also through a luminous
path that leads me to her heart!
I want to enter her kitchen to taste the delicious food
she prepared with her blessed hands.
I want to go into her bathroom to smell her herbs,
perfumes, powders and creams that she applies
on her freckles and classy moles, a mole after a mole.
I want to come into her bedroom to stretch in her bed
and wrap myself in the sheets that smell like her breath.
I want to open her wardrobe that smells of her
sexy garments also!
I want to see her library and the books lined up there.
I want to see her papers and the last poems she wrote.
I want to see her vases and their young red roses.
I want to contemplate in her garden and among the yellow
dandelion flowers which flirt under the warmth of her sun.
I want to see her swing, her rocking chair, her wooden table
and the poems she radiates on the grass like dew drops here
and there.
I want to see the traces of her cigarettes,
press my lips against hers
and inhale the smoke straight from her lung.
I want to kiss her eyes
and whisper the yearning in her ears.
I want to look attentively at her from the highest hair on the
tip of her head down to the last nail in her toe.
I want to lay her head on my knee and caress
the lobe of her ear.
I want to grab her fingers and apply polish on her nails.
I want to comb her golden hair and trim her eyebrows with
the experience of an old gardener.
I want to line her eyes and apply my blood as a lipstick on
her lips.
I want to choose what she is wearing today, tomorrow and
the day after as well.

I want to get on a fast train and meet her by chance again,
forty dreams ago from now and fifty pains in the heart
since then!
Yet, I will not let her go this time, and I will not get my
heart wounded with the razors of losing her.
I will be a crazy guest by her craziness,
and a fully authorized citizen in her heart!

I'm Trying!

Since last April, I have been trying, Camellia, to turn you to ashes in my heart. There you have been just more burning fire. I'm trying to close my eyes so that I don't see your light; yet my eyes, open or closed, end up not being able to see the light of any women other than you. I'm trying to avoid all the paths to you; yet I see myself nowhere other than on the paths to you. I'm trying to head towards a direction opposite to yours; I don't know what power drags my legs toward you. I'm trying to dispose all of my memories with you into the well of forgetfulness; unwillingly, I see them lightening in my memory. I'm trying not to utter your name at all; I see it only glistening on my tongue. But I will make you a promise: I will forget you! No, no, no . . . I'm not making any promises to you . . . I'm not making any promises to you. Goodbye for now . . . I miss hugging you so much!

By the Rhine River

He has nothing to say.
Hands in pockets,
Heart on his chest.
No, he left his heart on purpose in the heart of
A crazy woman.
She kept writing about her little Sisyphus
And about the stones with their bright colors
That God granted.
He has nothing to say, especially now.
He walks alone, all by himself
On rough roads,
Shirtless,
Bareheaded,
With wounded tongue.
He whistles with a wounded tone
And his eyes are on the careless cloud that sways
Over the Rhine!
He walks mindlessly.
No thoughts,
No exhaustion.
He asks all the beings he encounters on his way,
On the paths where he may retrieve his heart
From the heart of that crazy woman.
She was putting the stones on top of each other
And making high towers.
Then she would break them down
With a slight gasp from her little finger
So that the smile would appear
On the face of her little Sisyphus
With whom children refuse to play!
His heart grows in her heart!

The same way the heart of her Sisyphus is growing
In the heart of the hidden stone in his pocket.
Mystified, he is wondering,
What does she have to do with it?
What does her heart have to do with it?

A Toast to Chengdu

In Chengdu,
after midnight, poets were sneaking
to bars and taverns that hustle and bustle with life.
They were giving a toast to Chinese women and men
who were laughing with pure hearts all the time.
Poets were laughing along with them
with pure hearts as well.
Glasses would not stop, again for another
and another round!
They were giving a toast to China's great poets:
A toast to Du Fu
A toast to Li Bai
A toast to Su Shi
A toast also to Jidi Majia.
They were giving a toast
to Kuan Zhai street, Chengdu's long vivid braid,
to magnificent Chinese songs,
to China's astonishing drunks,
to the short Chinese singer while she was applying perfume
on her lips.
Toasts to each other as well!
Around three in the morning,
they were going back to their room in Xinhua hotel
and had the last glass, with a toast
to the marvelous Chengdu, of course!
And they fell asleep like the dead
that will wake up, no doubt.

The Rain in Chengdu

In Chengdu,
rain is always awake, never asleep;
straw clouds come side to side,
dark, they condense
above the head of lofty buildings.
It drizzles in showers,
then pours down like enormous tears.
Yet interestingly enough,
sidewalk vendor women
keep promoting their goods.
The homeless holds for his tiny dog
a hand-fan, colorful like peacock feathers.
Buddha comes out of the temple humbled,
receives his share of the wetness.
The green lion does not conceal itself out of sight,
nor does the golden elephant that sits on the
white marble pillar in the square.
Nobody cares for rain,
and life walks down wet,
hatless in the streets.
But it is strange
that, occasionally,
rain packs his bags and goes out of sight
like a thief who had committed a big felony.
The sun,
all of a sudden,
shines with laughter
high in the blue,
and embraces the face of Chendgu
with warmth and light.

The Chinese Poet, Paul Celan and I

When he learned that I come from Germany,
the Chinese poet from Beijing
told me about Paul Celan
with unmatched delight.
He celebrates me as if I am a twin of Celan.
He tells me about his ambiguous poetry
and evident grandiosity.
I share his opinion, of course!
And I push him to go on with this topic.
Yet, suddenly, he asks me:
"Have you read 'Poppy and Memory'?"
Of course, my friend!
"Have you read his poem about the philosopher
of the Black Forest and his small village Todtnauberg?"
Of course, my friend!
"Have you read his great letters to Ingeborg Bachmann?"
Of course, my friend!
I tell him, let's not talk about the Seine river
and the Mirabeau bridge, the seducer!
He gets it.
He thinks for a moment.
Suddenly, he chants a poem in Chinese,
by Celan, I guess.
With a childlike thrill, I applaud him.
My heart applauds him as well.
Shortly after, we get off the car that took us
from the airport to the Xinhua Hotel.
By the hotel door, I give him a warm handshake.
Each of us goes in to his room
while the soul of Celan keeps flapping
over the sky of Chengdu like an extraordinary bird of light.
Maybe that soul of light was tempting the imagination

of the Chinese and the Kurdish poet
to write poems like daisy flowers;
or maybe that soul wanted it
as a necklace of love and gratitude
for the neck of the grand Chengdu.

A Rose for the Heart of Life

Translations by

Norddine Zouitni

Kurdistan

On the veranda of my heart,

Blood drops stood alert

Like wounded lionesses

While out of the earth

A lily with sad lips sprang up.

Down ran my blood in unison with my heartbeats.

It hugged the sad face of the lily,

Turning its lips purple.

There, a homeland was born: Kurdistan.

Afrin

The city of God on my heart's shoulders

Afrin, God's last masterful kick in the face of nature
A colorful tulip, grown under the breasts of
Stubborn mountains
A stone tablet, fallen from the eye of legends
Sweet words on the lips of skylarks, pigeons
And grouses . . .
Afrin, the spoilt Gazelle of Kurds
Whose hair is plaited with the laughter of olive trees,
Sumac, wheat ears, and vineyards
A woman, asleep in her lover's bed while her plaits
Are being defiled by hissing vipers
And the whims of tyrants
Afrin, mud houses, coated with henna, raisins and
Grandmothers' eyelashes
A story and a legend, written in the ancestors' language,
Heavy with memories and longing
Afrin, a trifle in the mouth of politicians, pedants,
Dodgers, and renegades
Afrin, an ocean, surrounding earth like a ring
A record, written with the forearm
The Phoenix points its beak in all directions
And says: Those are the borders of our hearts,
The rhetoric of our people
Those are the frontiers of our love, our everlasting love.

The Heartbreak

I have no homeland on the walls of which I can scribble
with children's chalk: "Long live my homeland!"
I have no homeland to sip in the morning
with my morning coffee,
at sunrise as warmth covers it.
I have no homeland that can breathe through my lungs,
and through whose lungs I can in turn breathe,
whose husky voice I can be
and which can in turn my voice be.
I can be the villain, the brawler, the rebel, the stubborn
while it is the sage, the judicious, the gracious,
the generously souled.
I have no homeland to write on the brass door plate
of one of its houses:
"This is the house of Hussein Habasch.
Welcome, friends!"
I have no homeland in whose pubs I can get drunk
until very late at night,
on whose streets I can hang around.
And in my heart, it can in turn hang around.
A homeland I can wear and which in turn can wear me,
a homeland I can gently reproach,
which in turn can gently reproach me,
just like friends.
I have no homeland.

Sad Kurdish Poems

I read sad Kurdish poems.
Yesterday, I saw a dead bird
Lying on the roadside.
I carried it gently into my palm
Which I curved inward like a nest.
I took it to the cemetery
And buried it in a tiny grave shaped like my heart.
Today, I saw a crushed rose.
I picked its torn petals very gently
And put them on the bird's epitaph,
The one I saw yesterday
Lying dead on the roadside.
I'll probably carry on
Reading sad poems.

The Ant's Shoes

1
Sparrows chirp nervously
A fearful sun
The viper messes up the nests
The hatchlings cry out for help

2
Some worms eat into tree trunks
Other worms weave silk threads

3
Early morning
People, asleep
The fragrant scent of daffodils
Fills up the air

4
Leaves falling off profusely
Autumn is giving up its last breath

5
Earth is crying out
Her shouts drown out my moaning
What did you, villains, do to her?

6
A lake on top of a high mountain
The amazed lark wonders,
How did water climb to such rugged height?

7
On the face of the lake
The duck leads its young
The lioness gazes at her and says:
She's worthy of leadership indeed!

8
A wild flower grew on the river's edge
A butterfly sucks the nectar from the flower's lips
The river flows forever
The nectar won't run out

9
In the green fields
The cow chews grass
Milk for kids' growth
Dung for soil fertility

10
He named the fish "a longtime companion"
He was a real sailor

11
The dragonfly runs away from the wasps
And hides inside their hole
So fortunate are the wasps!

12
The fox grinds his teeth
The foolish hen is around the corner

13
A small breeze blew
And said, I am the wind's spoilt daughter

14
He bought pants without pockets
He knows, he doesn't need them at all!

15
The ant's shoes are tiny, so tiny
That wherever she treads
The ground stays clean

16
Spring spreads out its fragrance over the Earth
The sparrow laughs
And says: So lovely are God's gifts!

17
The cracked mountain
Will never roll down
It will turn into a rubble

18
In the house, about to fall,
The stones won't crumple in
But the hearts of those that built it will

19
My dad asks the rooster: Why do you crow?
The rooster answers: Just a habit, passed down
From father to son

20
The fox's heartbeats point
Towards the chickens' cackling

A Rose for the Heart of Life

Translations by

Jawad Wadi

Praises

We praise the age
So as not to overtake us.
We slightly snatch
Its biography
Or its vision
To lean on the vaults
Of the slumber,
Lighting an ambler thicket
For its dream.
The age is seduction and slander
As the wind said.

We praise the sea.
We praise its color,
Its dye and the comrade
Of its way.
We praise the sharks
So as not to steal
Our bodies
And our thrown garments
In the depth of the haze as well.
Oh you, dolphins,
Come, and you too, carps!
You, the fluttering
Pleasures on fish scales,
Come to me.
Guard the water
From its sway,
And entertain
The ornaments of
The afflicted lamps,
Guard the pearls

From the loss
Of its state
And the gush
Of brightness' elixir.
The sea is
Desire and excitation
As the triangle said
From its pierced side.

We praise the air.
We praise its swift penetration
For the justice
In my fair hair
From the favor
Of its permanent places.
We praise the air
And its obscurity.
We decode the talisman
Of its dark, silent, plundered
And afflicted tongue
In the alluvium of speech.
The air is a gift
As the directions said.

We praise the flight and sparrows
To the boundaries
Of the lancets,
Leaving their feathers,
The caftans of the horizons
As the wings said.
When they were shedding their waving
On adieu-wildflowers . . .
The flight is confusion and insanity
As the beaks said.

We praise the fire.
The cheers are sliding
From ants' mouths.
Chairs of thrones
Close their wooden wombs.
The souls of beautiful girls
Who were killed
Are wandering
In the adits of a fizzle,
Knocking at the doors of nothingness.
And the fire is rolling
Its blazing ball
On the kings' oppression.
The fire is death and inflation
As destinies said.

We praise laudation itself.
Laudation is a sedition,
Rising and failure
As the sun said.

The Deficient Trinity
Gleamed at Its Full Welfare

For the hand on the hand
To complete
The absent hand
In the sixth ordeal,
The dust of resurrection
Flutters at Narcissus' bloom
From the king of the jungle.
In the trembled morning,
All the Psalms' groups
Wake up from their long trance,
Playing for the dust vision,
Laughter, and gloom,
More pleading than
Drones' call and tender sparrows.
Brimful glasses are tottering
To lead the deer
To the deficient trinity
For a welfare, yearning
For a mazing perfection,
Flaring up the remnants of love
With sanity in the heads,
And say:
Pick me and dance with me
On the waste gates.
Then shed me
In nonchalant villages
Which rise from
The sediment dawn.
When great dampness,
To be curved,
Fidgets in the

Galaxies of blazes
To flame the ocean garments,
Whenever the seas

Get closer to the body of eternity
To dip our sorrow in obscurity,
We hunt the eighth hand
And smear it deeply
With the kohl of handshakes
To open the shining cities;
And with exciting intimacy,
Alienation shines.
We get busy with
The mercury of wine.
So, as stars' shirts
Implore us
And pavements' veils as well,
We come with the
Eighth hand
And rub the dust
From the heart's strain.
Then we light up
A slot
Out of extinction,
Searching through the
Regions of illusion
For the treasure
Never to be soiled.
Wolves' treachery . . .
We remove fraud
And trickery
By extinction and air.
The faint celebrations flow
From the petals of flowers,
And passing butterflies

Fly the cocoons of inattention
In the empty places
For the eighth hand,
Turning like
The dragon's glowing
Towards unknown spaces,

For the eighth hand
Clouded with longing,
Escorting the Kurds' pain
And the wounds lying on the chest of the forests.

An Evening on the Rhine

The coldness scarifies
The shyness of the naked trees.
A woman is sunken
In her dark coat.
We move away.
There is only two of us,
She and I.
Step after step
While the rain
Enwraps the rest
Of the pale leaves
And the ships with cargos
Across the river,
The distance between us
Grows further
As well as
The electric bulbs.
Meanwhile,
They are embracing
Each other
By the water screen.
I am kissing her
For an embracing glow.
The grass shudders.
The Rhine is applauding
With colours
And is singing for us,
"Be happy!"
The rustle of the trees
Writes a green legend.
We talk to the river
In different mysteries.
What a lovely and brilliant
This evening is!

A Lover and a Lover

We were two
Only two
Passed the gate
Of our old city . . .
One was Jamshid
The other was Mam
One was looking for
A house, a homeland,
And a garden
The other was looking for
A woman and kissing
But the city
Harshly
Chased us
It chased us
Away and away
With whips
Made of lead.

The Fountain

The mother nurses her child,
Her bosoms are a fountain.
The female grants her love for free,
Her heart is a fountain.
The bird flies on the horizon,
Its wings are a fountain.
The pen is dancing on paper,
Its ink is a fountain.
The rolling head of the poet
In the center of the arena
Is a fountain.

Translation by

Hewa Habasch

Hussein Habasch

The Silence of the City During Corona

Last night, I went through the center of my city;
I went through it like going through a labyrinth of fear,
lifelessness and emptiness.
No human being,
No creation,
Nor was there a living trace to bring peace to my steps.
Only me and my shadow, and a few yellow lights
were together.
God, what anger has come to my precious city?
What the hell is this?
What is this disaster?
What is this indignation?
Why did this city that was full of movement and activity
become so empty and silent?
I took larger steps; I quickly reached the vast square.
I saw Beethoven – the master of silence, the city's
gate keeper and protector – still in his place.
With joy, I went towards him, greeting him warmly.
Slowly, calmness and peace have returned to me.
With confident and free steps, I returned to my home.

Translation by

Mohammad Helmi Rishah

Years Gone Like Death

Without waving its hand to say goodbye, o poor orphans,
the year nodded its head and went
    without a desire to extinguish.
Behold, a new year has come, and behold,
    it is opening its shoelaces.
It would like to sit on our chest for 365 days without
    mercy.
Welcome, New Year!
We know that sometimes you will fall upon us with love
    and tenderness,
And usually, you gift us wars and grief; we know this
    thoroughly!
But even so, we will say to you, welcome, dear guest!
With your cruelty, your softness, you are among us.
No matter what happens, we will never be mad at you,
    nor will we leave you.
So, welcome, welcome!
A year, gone; a year, comes.
And our age goes on without sins, without returning
    to its death.
A Happy New Year, then, o world!
O world . . . which aborts our dreams and kills them
    always!

Translation by

Margaret Saine

Hussein Habasch

The Tiger

When I was young,

I wanted to be a tiger with strong claws

To attack anyone who would block my path.

When I grew up, I wanted to be a tiger

Who would travel around the world without claws.

When I got old,

I wanted to be just a tiger

Or a tiger who has a house and a roof

To protect himself from the claws of tigers.

Translation by

Solara Sabah

I Don't Care How or Where I Die

I rest my head on the rock of the oblivion.
Like a chorus, I echo the saddest song as follows:
I don't care if I die poor
or poorer than the poorest people of the world.
My two children are eating apples
and chewing on pomegranate seeds.
This is most important!
I don't care if I die.
Then I will wake up, walking alone in my funeral.
I don't care if I never wake up.
My two children are whispering to each other
with joy and happiness
as if they were two lovers.
This is most important!
Sargon Boulus had passed away in Berlin alone
as he was always alone;
reeled in to the brink of death as if he was a drunken Angel.
He was sick.
As a forgotten Prince,
Kamal Sabti died in a sofa in his home in Holland.
Ageel Ali had passed away on a sidewalk
as if he was formed to be the crown of all the homeless.
Mahmoud al-Braikan was killed with the knife of a thief.
He was a lighthouse, guiding the pirates
to his penniless pockets.
Then why should I care if I die in a bar, ballroom,
cabaret or in the arms of a whore in a brothel?
My two children are eating French fries with mayonnaise.
This is most important!
I don't care if I die by drowning, burning, strangulation,
slaughter or by committing suicide with carbon monoxide,
like my sister Sylvia Plath.

I don't care if I am put to death on my birthday,
like my brother Dilshad Meriwani,
the strange angel of Kurdistan.
I don't care if I die hungry, imprisoned or under the wheels
of a reckless train, like my spiritual twin Attila József.
I don't care if I am murdered in the hands of a mob,
like Lorca, or hanged like Hasan Mutlak,
"Dabada" of Baghdad.
More importantly, my two children are okay!
And I write simple farewell love poems,
inspired by the flirtation of the waitresses
and the beautiful young girls, passing in front of the café.
My two children are playing.
My daughter is combing her Barbie's hair,
and my son is riding his tiny motorbike.
This is most important!
I don't care if I am stabbed with a treacherous knife
or given a dose of venom, like my uncle Socrates.
I don't care if my death occurs in Athens, Berlin, Beirut,
Damascus, London, Madrid or beautiful Washington!
Cities are similar.
Death is a wandering dog, prowling along the skylines.
My children are rolling a ball-like planet,
and they seem fascinated by it.
This is most important!
I don't care if I die homeless in exile, achy, sad or drunk
or stabbed by friends' tusks, like most poets.
It is important that in this moment
I'm listening to Maria Callas.
Deep down, my inner self is soaked
in her melodious voice!
And my two children are sleeping innocently, it's amazing.
This is most important!
I don't care if I stutter with a drool
or sail through the madness swirl,

like my companion Cioran,
roaming the night due to insomnia,
putting my fate in the hands of coldness and delirium.
My two children are smiling in their sleep,
dreaming, perhaps about birds or butterflies.
This is most important!
I don't care if I live or die!
It makes no difference!
Death is the departure of the soul.
I lost my soul a long time ago
in the forests of the oblivion.
Why should I care now?
I don't care!

epilogue

about the A uthor . . .

Hussein Habasch is a poet from Afrin, Kurdistan. He currently lives in Bonn, Germany. His poems have been translated into English, German, Spanish, French, Chinese, Turkish, Persian, Albanian, Uzbek, Russian, Italian, Bulgarian, Lithuanian, Hungarian, Macedonian, Serbian, Polish and Romanian. His poetic work has been published in a large number of international anthologies. His books include: *Drowning in Roses*, *Fugitives Across Evros River*, *Higher Than Desire and More Delicious Than the Gazelle's Flank*, *Delusions to Salim Barakat*, *A Flying Angel*, *No Pasarán* (in Spanish), *Copaci Cu Chef* (in Romanian), *Dos Árboles*, and *Tiempos de Guerra* (in Spanish), *Fever of Quince* (in Kurdish), *Peace for Afrin, Peace for Kurdistan* (in English and Spanish), *The Red Snow* (in Chinese), *Dead Arguing in the Corridors* (in Arabic), *Drunken Trees* (in Kurdish) and *Boredom of a Tired Statue* (in Kurdish). The author has participated in many international poetry festivals in numerous countries, including Colombia, Nicaragua, France, Puerto Rico, Mexico, Germany, Romania, Lithuania, Morocco, Ecuador, El Salvador, Kosovo, Macedonia, Costa Rica, Slovenia, China, Taiwan and New York City.

E: habasch70@hotmail.com

about the $\bigwedge$rtist . . .

Ahmed Kleige was born in 1964 in Aleppo, Syria. He has completed college with a degree in chemistry, but never worked in that field. He began to paint instead and studied at the Fahti Fine Arts Center. Places where he lived and worked include Homs in Syria and Beirut in Lebanon. A few years ago, he fled to England where his family lives, but did not get any further than Nijmegen. It is there where he found shelter with friends and applied for an asylum. He has since been granted residence status in the Netherlands, and a home has been assigned to him, his wife and their three children in Maastricht.

Previous works of the artist have been acquired by The Ministry of Education and the Opera House in Damascus as well as numerous other cities around the world. One of his statues has been placed on the Ras Al Maten plane in Lebanon.

A Timeline for Ahmed Kleige

Graduation, Fathee Mouhamad of Plastic Arts school (Aleppo, 1987)

Member, Plastic Artists Syndicate in Damascus
Member, Arti-Shook Gallery in the Netherlands
Member, Foundation Taylor

Award, The Osama magazine Children's drawing award (1975)

Expositions:

Expositie Limburgse Kunstkring Kasteel Vliek (2019)
Expositie Gemeente Meerssen 75 jaar bevrijding (2019)
Gallery Rob van Rijn Maastricht (2019)
Annual Arti-Shook Exposition Den haag (2017)
Gallery Arti-shook Rijswijk Netherlands (2017)
Gallery Van Lueke Mense Netherlands (2016)
Gallery Janine Rubeiz, "Shattered Faces" (Beirut, 2013)
Gallery Naher Al Khaled Homs (2009)
Opera House Damascus, "Transhumances 2" (Damascus, 2008)
Gallery Zaman, "Transhumances" (Beirut, 2007)
Gallery Zaman, "Them" (Beirut, 2004)
American University, "Memories" (Beirut, 2003)
Gallery Zaman, "Glaring" (Beirut, 2002)
Symposium Ras Al maten (Lebanon, 2002)
UNESCO Palace (Beirut, 2000)

Links:

Muurschildering in Heerlen:
https://schunck.nl/agenda/ahmed-kleige/

Krant in Libanon:

www.lorientlejour.com/article/831831/ahmed-kleige-et-sandra-issa-la-memoire-dans-la-peau.html

TV interview:
www.youtube.com/watch?v=EOzA-Z0_j1E
Schilderijen:
www.youtube.com/watch?v=AwlHM-5J1Cw

TV-interview:
www.youtube.com/watch?v=Kc3R_x7Vsu8&t=87s

Expositie in Arnhem:
www.vanleukemensen.nl/kunstenaars/ahmed-kleige

Expositie in Wijchen:
www.youtube.com/watch?v=-YlsbuB2Qu8
www.gelderlander.nl/maas-en-waal/helpende-hand-naar-vluchtelingen-in-wijchen~ace89bae/115169870/

Lavina Meijer: (de schilder in dit filmpje is Ahmed Kleige)

www.youtube.com/watch?v=Ikn4B7jq6Ic

Inner Child Press

Inner Child Press is a publishing company founded and operated by writers. Our personal publishing experiences provide us an intimate understanding of the sometimes-daunting challenges writers, new and seasoned may face in the business of publishing and marketing their creative "Written Work".

For more information:

Inner Child Press

www.innerchildpress.com

intouch@innerchildpress.com

Inner Child Press International

'building bridges of cultural understanding'

202 Wiltree Court, State College, Pennsylvania 16801

www.ingramcontent.com/pod-product-compliance
Lightning Source LLC
Chambersburg PA
CBHW032059080426
42733CB00006B/336